THE OFFICIAL GAME GUIDE

HARPER
An Imprint of HarperCollinsPublishers

Adopt Me!: The Official Game Guide

Written by Craig Jelley

Copyright © 2024 Adopt Me!™
Uplift Games™
Visit playadopt.me and join the fun!
Ask a parent before going online.

All rights reserved. Manufactured in Italy.
No part of this book may be used or reproduced in any manner whatsoever without written permission except in the case of brief quotations embodied in critical articles and reviews. For information address HarperCollins Children's Books, a division of HarperCollins Publishers, 195 Broadway, New York, NY 10007.
www.harperchildrens.com

ISBN 978-0-06-331807-6

23 24 25 26 27 RTLO 10 9 8 7 6 5 4 3 2 1

Originally published in Great Britain 2024 by Farshore
First U.S. edition, 2024

Content in Adopt Me is regularly updated. Information in this book is correct as of October 2023.

ONLINE SAFETY FOR YOUNGER FANS

Spending time online is great fun! Here are a few simple rules to help younger fans
stay safe and keep the internet a great place to spend time:
- Never give out your real name – don't use it as your username.
- Never give out any of your personal details.
- Never tell anybody which school you go to or how old you are.
- Never tell anybody your password except a parent or a guardian.
- Be aware that you must be 13 or over to create an account on many sites. Always check the site policy and ask a parent or guardian for permission before registering.
- Always tell a parent or guardian if something is worrying you.

Stay safe online. Any website addresses listed in this book are correct at the time of going to print. However, HarperCollins is not responsible for content hosted by third parties. Please be aware that online content can be subject to change and websites can contain content that is unsuitable for children. We advise that all children are supervised when using the internet.

This book is produced from independently certified FSC™ paper
to ensure responsible forest management.

For more information visit: www.harpercollins.co.uk/green

CONTENTS

Welcome to Adoption Island 4
Orientation 6
First Steps 8
Eggs 101 10
Raising Pets 12
Parlor Pets 14
Common Pets 16
Uncommon Pets 18
Rare Pets 20
Ultra-Rare Pets 22
Legendary Pets 24
Neon Cave 26
Pet Fashion 28
Celebrations 30
Toil and Trouble 32
Grab a Bite 34
Supermarket 36
Moving In 38
The Neighborhood 40
Home Improvement 44
Moneymaker 46
Deals on Wheels 48
Showroom 50
Smart Trader 52
Pool Party! 54
Night in the Woods 56
Making Fun 58
Playtime! 60
Obby Lobby 62
Come Back Soon! 64

SIR WOOFINGTON

Why hello there, human!

Let me take this opportunity to welcome you to the haven of Adoption Island—the home of Adopt Me. Whether this is your first visit or you're a regular guest, there's always more to explore around here.

You can live any kind of life you want on Adoption Island—be it as an adult or a baby. Want to hatch and raise a pet? Well, you're in good company here. How about making a nice nest for you and your ever-expanding family? Then take a trip down to the Neighborhood, grab a plot of land, and start creating your dream home.

And if you've just stopped by for a ton of fun, we've got you covered too! Meet the locals, hang out with your friends, visit the playground and run the obbies, or visit one of the many shops or eateries to spend your hard-earned Bucks.

What are you waiting for? Browse through this handy guide to find out absolutely everything that Adopt Me has to offer you.

Enjoy your stay!

Sir Woofington

ORIENTATION

Jumping into a new game can sometimes be a little bit overwhelming, so let's take some time to show you everything you'll see on the screen and what it means. Once we've got that sorted, you can concentrate on having fun!

BUCKS COUNTER

This tells you how many Bucks—the Island's main currency—you currently have. You'll need Bucks to buy food, eggs, pets, toys, and basically everything else so try to keep your balance healthy. Turn to page 46 to find out how to earn more Bucks.

TASK BUBBLES

When your pet or baby needs something, a bubble will appear at the top of the screen telling you what to do. You can click on the bubble and it'll create a path to where you need to go!

BACKPACK

The backpack is an inventory of every item you own in Adopt Me, from food and pets to vehicles. Your things are split into categories so that you can easily find and equip the items you want, and you can even star items to add them to a special Favorites category.

STAR REWARDS

The Star Rewards system is a loyalty scheme, which gives you special stars for all the times you visit the island. This tab lets you spend the stars you've collected on limited-edition items that you won't be able to get anywhere else!

DRESS UP

A big part of Adopt Me is role-playing, so the Dress Up tab is great for creating looks for different roles. You can dress your avatar in different clothes that you can buy with Bucks, then save the outfit to a quick menu so you can change super-fast!

JOURNAL

This cute little scrapbook charts your collection of items, pets, vehicles, and more. It will be full of stickers of everything you own, and blank spaces for stuff you're missing from your collection. Hover over those blanks and you'll get info on what exactly you need to look for!

FRIENDS

Adoption Island is much better with friends. The Friends tab shows you all the friends you've added in the game. It lets you browse people nearby then add them if you've enjoyed hanging out! Remember: NEVER give out any personal information to people you don't know.

CREATE FAMILY

Once you've got friends, you can create a family with them using the Create Family button. After you've done this, you'll be able to invite people into your family so you can role-play and interact with their pets.

SHOP

If you are looking for something new, you can press the Shop tab to show all the deals that Adopt Me has to offer, from exclusive pets and vehicles to full bundles of homes, cars, and more!

FIRST STEPS

New arrivals to Adoption Island should swing by the Nursery first. Here you'll be able to pick up your very first egg, meet a couple of egg experts, and decide whether you want to explore the island as a parent or child ...

WHAT CAME FIRST?

When you first set foot on the island, you'll get to choose your first pet—either a Cat or a Dog. You'll also receive your very first egg—the Starter Egg, which will hatch into a random pet if you treat it well. But there are plenty more eggs to find ... for example, Sir Woofington sells the exclusive Royal Eggs.

EGGS GALORE

You can find pets in almost every corner of Adoption Island, but the Nursery is the only place you'll normally be able to find eggs. Search for Holly in the blue building and she'll sell you a Pet Egg. Meanwhile, Doug, located in the big red barn, will trade a Cracked Egg for some Bucks. In the clearing between Doug and Holly there's a giant gumball machine which dispenses exclusive eggs that change every few months!

VERY IMPORTANT ADOPTERS

You can access the VIP Room of the Nursery if you purchase a VIP Gamepass. Here you can get your hands on the Retired Egg, which can hatch exclusive pets, and the Golden Bone, which can net you a Legendary Chow-Chow pet. Plus, you'll find as much food and drink as you or your pet need!

ADOPTION CENTER

Meet Anna at the Adoption Center, where she takes care of the babies and pets waiting to be adopted. You can also put babies and pets in the cribs to be looked after. Use the Age-o-matic machine to switch your avatar between parent and baby.

BOARD YET?

The Pet Board in the Nursery area is a scrollable screen showing all the pets that you have, and how many you have left to discover!

EGGS 101

Lots of the pets that you can collect in Adopt Me start out as an egg, whether they're Common or Legendary. These mysterious ovoids can turn into many different things as long as you pick your egg wisely and hatch them with love.

The type of egg you have determines the type and rarity of pet you're likely to hatch. Let's take a look at some of the different eggs that are on the menu!

CRACKED EGG

Available From: Doug in the Nursery — $350

Probabilities:			
Common	45%		
Uncommon	33%	Rare	14.5%
Ultra-Rare	6%	Legendary	1.5%

PET EGG

Available From: Holly in the Nursery — $600

Probabilities:			
Common	20%		
Uncommon	35%	Rare	27%
Ultra-Rare	15%	Legendary	3%

RETIRED EGG

Available From: VIP Area of the Nursery — $600

Probabilities:			
Common	20%		
Uncommon	35%	Rare	27%
Ultra-Rare	15%	Legendary	3%

ROYAL EGG

Available From: Sir Woofington in the Nursery — $1450

Probabilities:			
Common	0%		
Uncommon	25%	Rare	37%
Ultra-Rare	30%	Legendary	8%

GOLDEN EGG

Available From: Star Rewards — 660 Stars / 180 Days Login

Probabilities:			
Common	0%		
Uncommon	0%	Rare	0%
Ultra-Rare	0%	Legendary	100%

DIAMOND EGG

Available From: Star Rewards — 660 Stars / 355 Days Login

Probabilities:			
Common	0%		
Uncommon	0%	Rare	0%
Ultra-Rare	0%	Legendary	100%

SEASONAL EGGS

As well as the eggs that you're able to get your hands on all year round, Adopt Me will also sometimes have seasonal events with special eggs that hatch into limited-edition pets! These events normally run around special holidays like Christmas, April Fools' Day, and Easter, so be sure to come back often to see what's on offer.

THE GUMBALL MACHINE

As if that wasn't enough, the Gumball Machine in the Nursery is also often restocked with new eggs. Each new egg has a different theme that offers a host of new and exotic pets—for example, from the Southeast Asia egg you can hatch a Komodo Dragon, while the Mythic Egg gives you the chance to hatch a Phoenix!

HATCHING EGGS

So now you have your dozens of eggs, how exactly do you hatch them? By taking very good care of them, of course! In Adopt Me, you can do this by completing the tasks that you see at the top of the screen. Turn to page 12 to find out more about the tasks you'll need to do to take care of your new best friend.

PRECIOUS EGGS

The Golden and Diamond Eggs hatch a Griffin, Dragon, or Unicorn in a special design. You can get these eggs through trading or Star Rewards, claimed for consecutive days of play!

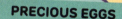

RAISING PETS

So you've hatched an egg and have an adorable little friend to play with ... but now what? Like every living thing, you need to ensure it's well taken care of by attending to its needs. Don't worry if you don't know how—just read these pages!

BASIC PET CARE

It doesn't matter whether your pet is Common or Legendary—they all have the same basic needs that you need to look after to help them grow big and strong. They'll let you know what they need when a task appears at the top of the screen, which will be one of four things:

HUNGRY		Pets like to run around, so you need to keep their energy up by feeding them. You can visit one of the food vendors—the Campsite, School, Green Groceries or Hotdog Stands—to feed your pet, or let them use a pet feeder in your house.
THIRSTY		Pets can quench their thirst in the Nursery's water fountain or from pet feeders at home or at the School. You can also grab drink items from stores like the Lemonade Stand and Coffee Shop, which are handy when you're out and about.
SLEEPY		If your pet is tired, you can put them to sleep in a pet bed or sleeping bag, which can be found at the School or Campsite, or by putting one in your house.
DIRTY		Pets have a tendency to get dirty, so make sure you wash them every now and again. You can clean your pets at your house, using a shower or a bathtub.

FUN WITH PETS

You'll also be given tasks when your pet wants a fun adventure! These tasks might require you to go to one of the island's exciting locations.

SICK		If your pet gets sick, then take it to the Hospital. You can cure your pet by talking to Doctor Heart, feeding it a Healing Apple, or using one of the medical beds.
BORED		If you're not having enough fun, the Bored task will send you to the Playground, where your pet will love tiring itself out on the various attractions.
SCHOOL		A well-trained pet is a happy pet, so it may compel you to visit the School. Visit the pet training room to tend to its needs and tick off this task.
SALON		Even pets need a glow-up once in a while, so for this task, take them to the Salon and see if they'll look better with a different color coat...
PIZZA PARTY		When you get the pizza party task, a home-cooked slice won't do the job, so you'll need to head down to the Pizza Shop to make your pet happy.
POOL PARTY		As if one party wasn't enough, your pet may want to visit the Pool to take a dip in the water and splash around with its pals too.
CAMPING		Your animal companions love to spend a night in the woods, so take a trip to the Campsite, toast some marshmallows, and strum some guitars to complete this objective.

TRICKS

As time passes and you complete tasks with your pet, it will grow up and be able to learn different tricks. Visit Pet Trainer Shane at the School and he can teach your pet up to six tricks depending on their age. The tricks can include sit, joyful, beg, and jump.

SPECIAL MOVES

Some special pets can learn unique tricks as well as the main ones. For instance, a fully grown Frost Dragon will be able to use the Frost Breath trick too.

PARLOR PETS

Now you know how to take care of your pet, it's time to have a bit of fun with them. Swing by the Pet Shop to meet Tom and pick up everything you need to keep your favorite pet happy. You might even see a couple of exclusive pets!

PET SHOP TOYS

What pet owner doesn't love to spoil their little furry friends—or much larger and less furry ones for that matter? The Pet Shop has everything you need to keep your pet pal entertained and all for very reasonable prices too!

TASTY TREATS

You can pick up both regular pet food and a pet treat from the Pet Shop, for 5 or 10 Bucks. A wise pet owner will stock up on lots of these before going on any long walks. Both items can be used once to complete the hunger task for a pet.

CHEW TOYS

Save your favorite slippers from the jaws of your pet with an entrancing chew toy. These come in key or shoe varieties and will keep your pet occupied with hours of gnawing until you pick it up again.

FETCH QUEST

If you want to let your pet stretch its legs, fins, or wings, then the Pet Shop has a ton of throwable toys to play with, including bones, flying discs, and balls.

SHORT LEASH

It can be a bit tricky to keep track of your pet. Luckily, you can buy a leash to use on your pet and create a bond between you.

PREMIUM PETS

Not only does the Pet Shop have everything you need for your pet, it also sells the pets themselves. The creatures available here can be purchased, but they're exclusive to the store and you won't even have to spend time hatching them! If you're interested, let's see which new friends you can take home.

SLOTH

R$ 199

Take it easy with this sleepy tree-dwelling mammal, who has giant claws to dig into trees.

ROYAL PALACE SPANIEL

R$ 299

Add a much-needed regal touch to your kennel with this majestic and obedient pet.

WINGED HORSE

R$ 800

With giant wings that can lift it high above any other steed, the Winged Horse is a sight to behold!

PAST PETS

Sometimes the pets on offer are taken out of rotation, but if you've missed the opportunity to purchase them, you can still get them through trading.

COMMON PETS

If you're just starting out on Adoption Island, the chances are your first few pets will be common ones. That doesn't mean they're any less cute and cuddly though. Let's take a look at some of the best pets from this tier.

MALEO BIRD

This exotic creature is normally found in the tropics of Indonesia, but luckily you can find it on Adoption Island too! It has distinctive yellow patches around its eyes, which will glow when upgraded to Neon.

Obtained By: Hatching from a Southeast Asia Egg, or trading

DOG

No family is complete without a four-legged furry friend, so be sure to snap up a Dog as soon as possible. The Dog can be hatched from the Starter Egg and is great at learning tricks. Good dog!

Obtained By: Hatching from a Starter Egg, Retired Egg, or trading

GROUND SLOTH

If you prefer a more laid-back pet, then the easy-going Ground Sloth might catch your eye. This sandy slowcoach has long, sharp claws for digging.

Obtained By: Hatching from a Fossil Egg, or trading

BULLFROG

Maybe cute and cuddly isn't your thing, but fear not: Adopt Me is full of cool, slimy amphibians too. This green critter will hop along behind you and jiggle around while it sits, looking for tasty flies.

Obtained By: Hatching from a Woodland Egg, or trading

BEST OF THE REST

ANT

OTTER

CAT

ROBIN

CHICK

STINGRAY

DUGONG

WOLPERTINGER

MOUSE

MALAYAN TAPIR

BALI STARLING

TASMANIAN TIGER

UNCOMMON PETS

If you're a bit luckier when you're hatching your eggs, you might get your hands on one of the uncommon pets. This tier of animal (and non-animal) pals is where things start to get really exciting. Have a look at some of our favorites below!

TRICERATOPS

Travel back millions of years to prehistoric times when dinosaurs roamed the planet ... and pick up a terrific Triceratops! It has spikes and frills all over its body, which glow brightly when it's upgraded to Neon.

Obtained By: Hatching from a Fossil Egg, or trading

SNOWMAN

This frosty friend was released during a winter event many years ago and has, surprisingly, not melted since. It has a carrot nose, stick arms, coal eyes, and buttons that you might see bobbling around the island any time of the year!

Obtained By: Trading only

KIRIN

This mythical creature looks like a cross between a giant deer and a tiny dragon. Based on a beast found in Chinese and Korean legends, it has antlers, a mane, and a flame-shaped tail.

Obtained By: Hatching from a Mythic Egg, or trading

PINK CAT

You have the choice of many feline friends in Adopt Me, but this one really stands out! The bright pink fur is colorful enough, but its whiskers, paws, and tail will all glow if it becomes Neon.

Obtained By: Hatching from a Pink Egg, or trading

BEST OF THE REST

PET ROCK | FENNEC FOX | BLUE DOG

RHINO BEETLE | MEERKAT | WILD BOAR

STEGOSAURUS | DINGO | BAT

2022 UPLIFT BUTTERFLY | GLYPTODON | ERMINE

RARE PETS

Now we're entering exclusive territory—the rare pets. This collection of colorful and kooky critters make their home everywhere from the water to the sky, but now you can bring them to your house if you're lucky enough!

FEESH

We've heard of treading water, but this takes it to another level. At first glance the Feesh seems normal, but it has two feet instead of a tail! This scaly friend looks like it'll be equally at home on land or in the water.

Obtained By: Trading only

HALLOWEEN EVIL DACHSHUND

This hellhound was released as part of a Halloween event, but don't let its appearance fool you—it's still a friendly pet to own. If you look past the glowing red eyes, horns, and pointed tail, it's just a normal sausage dog after all ...

Obtained By: Trading only

NARWHAL

Be careful when you're swimming in the waters around Adoption Island, because you might get poked by the Narwhal's giant tusk. The big pointy thing on its head is actually a tooth!

Obtained By: Hatching an Ocean Egg, or by trading

SASQUATCH

Legend says that the Sasquatch roams around the woodlands alone, taking food and supplies that it needs to survive. In reality, it's an adorable pet that you can take care of in Adopt Me!

Obtained By: Hatching a Mythic Egg, or by trading

BEST OF THE REST

WOODPECKER

GHOST WOLF

IRISH ELK

IBIS

MOON RABBIT

BASILISK

PTERODACTYL

POLAR BEAR

TARSIER

MERHORSE

SUMMER WALRUS

BEAVER

ULTRA-RARE PETS

You're going to be very fortunate if you start hatching any of the pets on this page! The Ultra-Rare creatures are some of the most wanted pets in Adopt Me, so make sure you keep an eye out for them when you're trading!

BUSINESS MONKEY

This suited pet is strictly business, yet somehow still incredibly cute. It wears a smart jacket and carries a briefcase around with its tail, which is certainly filled with important documents ... and probably bananas.

Obtained By: Trading only

LUNAR OX

Ring in the Chinese New Year with this member of the zodiac clan: the Lunar Ox. It's decorated in the traditional celebratory colors of red and gold, and has a golden collar and nose ring too.

Obtained By: Opening from an Ox Box, or by trading

WATER MOON BEAR

If you prefer your pets to be a bit cuddlier, look no further than the squishy and soft Water Moon Bear. This blue grizzly has a swirly pattern on its belly.

Obtained By: Opening from a Moon Bear Box, or by trading

KOMODO DRAGON

In real life, the Komodo Dragon can take down animals four times its size with a toxic bite. Luckily, biting isn't one of the tricks you can teach a Komodo Dragon in Adopt Me!

Obtained By: Hatching from a Southeast Asia Egg, or by trading

BEST OF THE REST

CORGI	HYDRA	WYVERN
SPACE WHALE	PINE MARTEN	TRAPDOOR SNAIL
GIANT BLUE SCARAB	CLOWNFISH	SABERTOOTH
PLATYPUS	ARCTIC FOX	SCARLET BUTTERFLY

LEGENDARY PETS

Finally we reach the rarest kind of pet that you can find in Adopt Me—the Legendary tier. These pets are harder to collect than any others. Let's take a look at some of the coolest ones you can get your hands on.

UNICORN

Who doesn't love a Unicorn? This rainbow-maned beauty was among the first batch of Legendary pets to be added to Adopt Me. Its Neon and Mega Neon forms have a glowing mane, tail, and hooves—how fancy!

Obtained By: Hatching a Retired Egg, or Trading

ADOPT ME!: STRAWBERRY SHORTCAKE BAT DRAGON

A combination of fruit, dessert, and animal, this is one of the most creative creatures that you can collect. Its candy-striped wings and strawberry-slice ears really set it apart from other pets.

Obtained By: Trading only

ANCIENT DRAGON

One for the traditional dragon fans! With its beard and ginormous horns, this winged beast is sure to gather a few looks from envious islanders.

Obtained By: Hatching a Cracked, Pet, or Royal Egg

AXOLOTL

This cute amphibious creature is a marvel, notable for its salmon pink color and the frilly gills on its head. Those frills glow brightly in its Neon and Mega Neon forms, as do the scales on its back.

Obtained By: Trading only

BEST OF THE REST

LAVA WOLF

QUEEN BEE

NAGA DRAGON

TREE KANGAROO

METAL OX

TIÓ DE NADAL

CAPRICORN

ROBO DOG

T-REX

DODO

BLACK CHOW-CHOW

GOLDHORN

NEON CAVE

Take a trip under the bridge between Adoption Island and The Neighborhood and you'll find the Neon Cave, where you can evolve your pets into amazing variants that will make you the envy of the island.

NEON INGREDIENTS

To create a Neon pet, you'll need FOUR of the same type of pet. The process will fuse their essences into one single, glowing Neon animal.

You'll also need to make sure that all of the pets that you're planning to use in the ritual are Full Grown. You can complete tasks to raise your pets up ready to make them Neon.

ANIMAL MAGIC

When you've got your four identical, full grown pets, enter the Neon Cave and you'll see a large mystical platform surrounded by four smaller ones. Place your pets onto the smaller platforms and the process will combine those four animals into a glowing Neon one!

WHAT IS NEON?

Neon pets behave exactly the same as a regular pet, and you can take care of them in all the same ways. The only difference is that their body will glow with magical energy from the Neon ritual. Every Neon pet has different parts that glow in multiple colors.

BASIC

NEON

GLOW UP

Surely an extraordinary luminous pet is enough for you now. No? Well, you're in luck because you can also upgrade Neon pets to Mega Neon versions. The process is exactly the same—put four identical Neon pets in the smaller circles and they'll merge into a Mega Neon variant that will cycle through glowing colors instead of having just one.

TALK OF THE TOWN

Now you know how to get your paws on a Neon or Mega Neon pet, let's take a look at a few of the coolest creatures you can collect for some added motivation!

NEON CERBERUS

NEON EMPEROR GORILLA

NEON SNOW OWL

NEON AXOLOTL

NEON ZEBRA

NEON ICE GOLEM

NEON DANCING DRAGON

NEON FALLOW DEER

NEON CLOWNFISH

NEON BAKU

PET FASHION

You can't change what your pet pal looks like, but you can give it some awesome bling so it stands out on Adoption Island. The Accessory Shop gives you the chance to dress your pet friend with dozens of cool, creative items.

STOCK SWAP

The accessories on the mannequins change twice a week, on Tuesday and Saturday. Visit frequently to make sure you don't miss out on a fashion bargain!

ACCESSORIZE!

Take a trip to the pirate-themed Accessory Shop and you'll see a few different items on display (on dog mannequins of course!) that you can purchase outright. These items range from crowns and earrings to backpacks and wings. They all have different rarities—just like pets do—so keep an eye out for rare and legendary items!

CHESTS

As well as the accessories that are on display, you can also purchase one of two chests, each of which will reward you with a random accessory when you open them.

STANDARD CHEST

 105

Probabilities:			
		Common	60%
Uncommon	30%	Rare	7.5%
Ultra-Rare	2%	Legendary	0.5%

REGAL CHEST

 300

Probabilities:			
		Common	20%
Uncommon	50%	Rare	20%
Ultra-Rare	8.5%	Legendary	1.5%

FASHION SHOW

There are hundreds of different accessories to collect and dress your pet up with. Let's look at some of the most creative ones you can get your hands on.

AXE GUITAR

BEAR WINTER HAT

CANDY CORN HAT

CHRISTMAS HAT

CUPCAKE SHOES

DRAGONFLY FAIRY WINGS

EGYPT CROWN

GHOST KITTY BACKPACK

ICE CROWN

LEAF MUSTACHE

LEANING CAKE

MAPLE LEAF CAPE

PRIDE GLASSES

RABBIT NOSE

SPIDERWEB CROWN

WOOL BEARD

29

CELEBRATIONS

Hang around Adoption Island for a while and you'll see that events from all around the world are celebrated here. Let's see what's on Adopt Me's calendar! Which ones will you celebrate this year?

LUNAR NEW YEAR

The first event of the year is full of lanterns, luck, and many more lunar influences. In 2023, Adoption Island hosted a game where you had to find lanterns hidden all around the island. You could then trade them for exclusive pets, lunar accessories, and even a Crescent Moon Car!

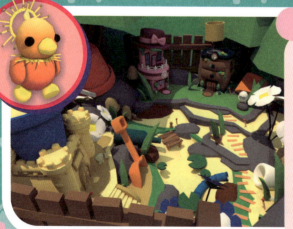

SPRING FESTIVAL

When spring has sprung, there are minigames and egg hunts to take part in all across the isle! These are normally themed around baby animals and blooming flowers. And of course there's spring swag to collect too, like the Tulip Stroller and Flower Beret.

PRIDE

In 2022, Adopt Me hosted its first Pride event, which celebrated the diversity of the LGBTQ+ community and gave the people of Adoption Island another way to express their individuality. There were dozens of flags added as items, a whole host of rainbow pet accessories, and even a special magic carpet vehicle that left rainbows in its wake!

HALLOWEEN

The spooktacular Halloween Event offers bucketloads of Candy to be won in scary minigames, which can be exchanged for petrifying pets, terrifying toys, and much more.

WINTER

Bringing the year to a close as the snow begins to fall, the Winter event is a fitting frosty finale. In 2022, the island played host to snowball fights, reindeer races, and ice skating. There was even an advent calendar with a bunch of freebies too!

TOIL AND TROUBLE

There's something magical brewing high above Adoption Island. If you can make your way to the clouds, you'll find Sky Castle, which stocks a variety of unusual potions that can be consumed by you or your pet. Make sure you check the labels first ...

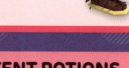

GETTING THERE

There are a few different ways to get to the Sky Castle. The easiest one is to pay five Bucks to ride the hot air balloon that shuttles players back and forth from the island. However, you can use a toy, like a propeller, to reach the castle, or fly on the back of a pet. "How do you get a flying pet?" I hear you ask ... just keep reading!

SIGHTSEEING

Go to the back of the castle and you'll find a rope that you can use to bungee off the floating island! You can also buy chests which hold a fancy pair of wings for your pet.

POTENT POTIONS

Now for the main attraction—the magical elixirs. You don't need to get your hands on a potion to fully enjoy Adoption Island, but they will make life a little more ... unusual. Let's see what's been brewing!

BIG HEAD POTION

 10

EFFECT: Consume this mystical liquid and it'll make your head grow to an inhuman size. Does it affect your abilities? No. Is it funny to see you and your friends with humongous heads wandering around the island? Absolutely.

HYPERSPEED POTION

40

EFFECT: If this pink potion passes your lips, your legs will be enchanted with an insane energy that makes you move a little bit faster. If that's not enough, the effects increase with every bottle, so you can drink more and more until you're zooming about at 100mph!

ANTI-GRAVITY POTION

99

EFFECT: Much like the Hyperspeed Potion, the effects of the Anti-Gravity one also increase with every dose. This time, the potion reduces how much gravity can affect you, allowing you to jump to inhuman heights!

GROW POTION

395

EFFECT: If enlarging your head isn't severe enough for you, grab a green Grow Potion to increase the size of EVERY body part. Like the Big Head Potion, you can only receive the effects of a Grow Potion once, so no growing to the size of a building!

TRANSLUCENT TEA POTION

600

EFFECT: There's nothing in this bottle! Oh, wait. The potion is see-through just like the glass! The Translucent Tea Potion is one for your pet and makes it slightly more invisible each time. Feed a pet five of these, and you'll only be able to see their eyes.

RIDE-A-PET POTION

R$ 150

EFFECT: It doesn't matter whether your pet is a mouse or a dragon, because this horse-shaped potion will make it possible to ride them around like you would a car or motorbike! It's very handy for getting around and improving the bond between owner and pet.

GRAB A BITE

All this travel around Adoption Island must have made you hungry. Luckily, there is an assortment of cafés and snack bars where you and your pet pals can replenish your energy right away. Here are two of the best snack places in town!

ICE CREAM SHOP

Look for the building that resembles a dropped ice cream cone and you'll find the home of glorious frosty treats. Adopt Me!: Elsa is the patron of the Ice Cream Shop and will get you a delicious cooling snack on a summer's day.

SELF SERVE

Once you've purchased a cone, you can stack it with up to three scoops of the seven available flavors. You can't put any more on or it'll collapse, but there's no rule to say you can't have a second cone ... or a third.

PICK UP A PENGUIN

The Ice Cream Shop also allows you to befriend a frosty pal. Here you can buy a Golden Goldfish and you'll be able to get your hands on a King Penguin. You might even get a Legendary Diamond King Penguin.

PIZZA SHOP

If you're looking for something that will fill you up a little more, stop by the Pizza Shop. This busy restaurant has soft dough, gooey cheese, and all the toppings you could ever ask for. Maybe you could even earn yourself a crust ...

GRAB A SLICE

Sit down at one of the booths and check out the menu before choosing one of the four delicious specialities. Order from the counter and the friendly staff will speedily summon your pizza treat.

PIZZA PARTY

At the Pizza Shop you can remedy the Pizza Party ailment that sometimes afflicts your pets. Spending a while hanging out here with your pet will make them full and happy once again.

JOB HUNT

If you'd rather get your hands doughy, you can get a job at the Pizza Shop! You can be a waiter, chef, or manager and you'll get paid in Bucks for making pizzas, delivering them to tables, or making sure the shop keeps working smoothly!

35

SUPERMARKET

Adoption Island will keep you very busy, so you might not always have the chance to drop by a restaurant. However, take a detour to Green Groceries and you can stock up on some local produce that you can eat on the go.

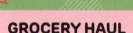

STOCKING UP

Look out for a building with slanted green roofs near the Campsite and you'll find Green Groceries, which has aisles of food that you can buy. There's a secret entrance to the Farm Shop in one of the fridges, which sells a special item to get an exclusive pet. Very cool.

BUG HUNT

Go through that fridge portal and you'll arrive in the Farm Shop, where you can obtain a special Diamond Lavender item for sale. You can scoop some up, then throw it to catch one of three different Ladybug pets.

GROCERY HAUL

There are dozens of food items around Adoption Island that you can feed to your pet, but none of them are fresher than what Green Groceries has to offer.

WATER 1

There's nothing better to quench thirst and quash the risk of dehydration than a fresh drink of water.

CHOCOLATE MILK 2

If water is a bit too plain, or you just fancy having a little treat, Chocolate Milk will resolve the Thirst ailment just as well as H20.

HOTDOG 2

For just a couple of Bucks, you can get your hands on what is basically a full meal to eat on the go! Bun? Check. Meat? Check. Too much mustard? Check!

APPLE 1

If you just can't wait for the apples to start falling from trees, Green Groceries has crate after crate of the healthy snack.

CHEESE 2

Why would anyone choose another food when you can chow down on a big, tasty wedge of cheese?

WATERMELON 2

Nothing is more refreshing to eat when the sun is shining than a giant wedge of watermelon.

RASPBERRY PIE 3

This delicious raspberry pie is hot and fresh out of the oven and a main attraction of Green Groceries.

HAM 3

If you'd prefer to eat like a caveperson, grab one of these giant hunks of ham and chomp on it like a meaty lollipop.

MOVING IN

It's about time we took a trip to the Neighborhood, where visitors to Adopt Me can settle down and make a home of their own. You'll need somewhere to stay with your gang of new pet pals after all!

STAKE YOUR CLAIM

Your house is where you'll spawn every time you enter Adopt Me, so you'll be visiting a lot. If it's your first time in the game, you'll start out in a Tiny Home, which is the cheapest, simplest house on offer. However, if you want to upgrade, you can sell it and purchase something bigger and better. Turn the page to see what other homes are on offer…

VISITING FRIENDS

Once you're happy with the house you've built, you can also customize it with furniture and decorations to make it unique. If you need inspiration, take a stroll around the Neighborhood and you'll be able to walk into unlocked houses to see what they've done with their place. Then go back to yours and get your DIY on.

SAFETY FIRST

If you don't want anyone to see your masterful interior decoration before it's ready, then you can press the lock button at the top of the screen to make sure no one can enter your house. You can tell which houses are unlocked because the doors will open when you get close!

HOUSE FLIPPER

You can remove any house that you buy and build on your land, and even get some money back for it, but be careful—all of the decorations and furniture that you've put in that house will also disappear in the sale! Better make sure you've got the budget for a ton of furniture before you move into your new house!

PARTY POOPER

You can throw a Party in most houses, but not all of them. The Tiny Home and Family Home are unable to host Parties, but any other house can become party central!

PARTY TIME

Celebrate your arrival in the Neighborhood by throwing a housewarming Party! Interact with the mailbox outside of your house to set up an invitation, which will be sent to all your neighbors. Guests will be able to drop by for the next ten minutes to hang out with their newest neighbor, and even give the Party a rating at the end.

THE NEIGHBORHOOD

As you wander through the Neighborhood, you'll see houses of all shapes and sizes dotting the skyline. Don't let jealousy get to you though, because you too can own one of these amazing homes! Let's see what's on offer.

PIZZA PLACE

Stories: 2   **Parties:** Yes   500

DESCRIPTION: Fresh out of the oven is the Pizza Place—part home, part delicious food factory. The customisable exterior can change colors to suit the owner, and will also feature your character's face on the front when you build it. The interior has all the equipment and ingredients you need to make an endless supply of pizza.

TREEHOUSE

Stories: 1   **Parties:** Yes   800

DESCRIPTION: Get closer to nature—so close that you're actually inside it—with the Treehouse. Easily accessible by a staircase that wraps around the tree's trunk, the cozy home is situated just underneath the canopy, providing great views of the surrounding area as soon as you step out the door.

FAIRY HOUSE

Stories: 3   **Parties:** Yes   💲 1100

DESCRIPTION: Nobody said that a home needs to be a house. Set yourself apart from your neighbors with the quaint Fairy House, which is a gigantic multi-purpose mushroom with windows and doors carved into the exterior. You can also change the color of the mushroom cap to make your place very easy to spot on your street.

PIRATE SHIP HOUSE

Stories: 2   **Parties:** Yes   💲 1600

DESCRIPTION: Shiver me timbers! If ye must be a land-lubber then there be only one house to choose—the Pirate Ship House. This impressive hull is no shipwreck, and will be the perfect place for any seadog to relax. It even comes furnished with pirate-themed decorations like a pirate ship bed!

SCARY HOUSE

Stories: 4   **Parties:** Yes   💲 1800

DESCRIPTION: It might not be the most inviting home, with its run-down exteriors and eerie glowing windows, but the Scary House will be snapped up in no time at all. If you can look past the dead trees and general bad vibes, there's plenty of space inside for a growing family and a nice front porch where you can give warning to any unwary visitors ...

GINGERBREAD HOUSE

Stories: 2   Parties: Yes

 1850

DESCRIPTION: Perfectly suited to those with a sweet tooth, the Gingerbread House is (obviously) made from gingerbread, with icing details on the roof and walls and a snowy surrounding garden. It's the perfect place to live, if you can resist eating it for long enough that is ...

FUTURISTIC HOUSE

Stories: 2   Parties: Yes

 2500

DESCRIPTION: For the more modern house-hunter, we have the Futuristic House. Its sleek exterior continues indoors, where you'll find a couple of bedrooms, a bathroom, a kitchen, and a very nice pool. The large, long balcony is also the perfect place to host Parties on a warm evening.

BIODOME HOME

Stories: 2   Parties: Yes

 2750

DESCRIPTION: Bring the inside outside, or the outside inside, with this ingenious Biodome Home. Entering the front door will take you to a beautiful open space under the dome, which is great for your pets to run around in. Somewhere in the lush expanse, you'll also find a simple two-story home, but you'll barely want to go indoors.

ROYAL PALACE

Stories: 2   Parties: Yes

$ 2750

DESCRIPTION: Live like a king, queen, prince, or princess in the regal Royal Palace. As you would expect from such a stately home, the exterior is adorned in intricate gold detail, and there's an abundance of space inside and out, perfect for throwing elegant balls or extravagant garden parties.

LUXURY APARTMENTS

Stories: 6   Parties: Yes

$ 8000

DESCRIPTION: Do you have lots of friends who frequently come to stay? Consider buying the Luxury Apartments and you'll no longer need to set them up on the sofa! The most expensive property on the market has six separate apartments, each with its own balcony, plenty of parking space, and a pool in the basement.

NO PARKING

You can't spawn a vehicle inside any of the houses, except for the Sandbox Island, the Racetrack House, and the Mountain House.

HOME IMPROVEMENT

So you've chosen your favorite house, visited the neighbors for inspiration, and have Bucks to spare ... it's about time you put your personal stamp on your property. Use edit mode to get decorating!

EDIT MODE

Changing the interior of your house is super simple. When you're in your house—or a house you have permission to edit—just press the EDIT button at the top of the screen and it'll bring up options to change WALLS, FLOORS, and STUFF. These three options will let you customize almost every part of your house with ease.

Edit House

Stuff   **Walls**   **Floors**

WALLS AND FLOORS

First decide what your ceilings and floors are going to look like. Think of it as a base layer for all the decorations you're going to put in there. You can apply wallpaper and carpets to individual floor tiles so you can create complex patterns even with these simple features.

STUFF

Once you've sorted out the walls and floors for all your rooms, it's time to get creative with the decoration. The STUFF option contains all the pieces of furniture that you can place in your house, from pet bowls and rugs to four-poster beds and DJ booths!

44

THE BEST STUFF

1950S TV

CANDY CHAIR

CAVEMAN FRIDGE

DRIFTWOOD JAR LAMP

GRAVESTONE PET BED

GUMBALL MACHINE CRIB

JAPANESE TEA TABLE

MELTED ICE CREAM BED

PREMIUM FIRE PIT

PUMPKIN WATER BOWL

RAINBOW BED

ROYAL CHANDELIER

SMALL ISLAND TREE

SMALL TENT

SPIDERWEB BED

TREASURE CHEST

MONEYMAKER

You'll know by now that making your dream home, owning a car, and taking care of your collection of pets isn't free, so it's time to look at how to line your wallet. Don't worry—it's very easy and very fun too!

PET CARE

The easiest way to earn a little bit of money is just to take care of your pet. The bubbles that appear at the top of the screen will all show a reward, in Bucks, for completing that task and tending to your pets' needs. And you were going to do that anyway!

NINE TO FIVE

There are some spots around Adoption Island where you can pick up a part-time job if you really want to get the money rolling in. The Pizza Shop has three jobs available that will reward you for making or delivering pizzas, or you can groom pets at the Salon.

SELF-EMPLOYED

If working for someone else isn't really your thing, you can go it alone with one of the stalls or vehicles that earn you money. The Lemonade, Hot Dog, and Cotton Candy stands can be pitched anywhere for you to sell snacks, or you can hop in the Ice Cream Truck to sell gelato on the go! You can get paid to drive people around the island if you have one of the Taxi vehicles.

MONEY DOESN'T GROW...

If you're looking for a bit of decoration in your house, consider the Money Tree. This golden plant will give you up to 100 Bucks a day and costs only 1450! You can make your money back in just over two weeks before it all turns into profit!

CASH FLOW

As part of the Daily Reward feature, you'll also receive money for the first few days of a login streak. It starts with just 25 Bucks on day one, but reaches 200 on the fourth day. In total, you'll receive 375 Bucks for a four-day login streak.

PAY TO PLAY

You can also convert real money into Bucks whenever you need a top up. Just be aware that buying Bucks or Premium Items costs real-life money and so you should always make sure you have the bill payer's permission.

25

200

375

DEALS ON WHEELS

You might have already noticed, but Adoption Island and the Neighborhood are HUGE! It can take a while to navigate on foot, but if you visit the Vehicle Dealership, you can get a set of wheels to speed up your travels.

VEHICLE DEALERSHIP

Visit Rich at the Vehicle Dealership to spend your hard-earned Bucks. Whether you want to go by land, sea, or air, Rich has got you covered. All you need to worry about is where you're going to jet off to in your new set of wheels.

SPAWNING VEHICLES

Once you've acquired a vehicle, you'll be able to spawn it anywhere you need it—apart from inside buildings, of course. Open up your Backpack and select the Vehicles inventory to show all the vehicles that you own. Select the one you want to ride and press equip!

PARKING SPACES

You can spawn your vehicle in most open spaces, but if you have the Millionaire Mansion, you'll have a parking space in front of your home to show off your sweet ride. You can also spawn a vehicle through the portal of the Sandbox Island house!

BICYCLE

 75

SEATS: 1
Use pedal power to get yourself around the island with the basic bicycle.

MOTORBIKE

400

SEATS: 1
This classic motorbike is perfect for getting riders from A to B.

CLASSIC BOAT

 2750

SEATS: 8
Set sail with up to seven pals on the Classic Boat.

TANDEM BICYCLE

300

SEATS: 2
Many feet make light work, so get a friend to join you on a cycle to your destination.

SPORTS BIKE

700

SEATS: 2
There's real horsepower packed into this sleek sports bike, and a buddy can hop on too!

FAMILY CAR

900

SEATS: 4
A sensible ride for a family of adults, babies, and a few pets.

OPEN TOP SPEEDER

1800

SEATS: 2
If you like to feel the wind in your hair on the open road, this Speeder is for you.

CLASSIC HELICOPTOR

3500

SEATS: 4
Take to the skies and arrive in style with this cool ride.

SHOWROOM

Vehicles have been around since Adopt Me was released, so you'll find dozens around the island away from the Vehicle Dealership. Let's have a look at some of the coolest ones that you can collect, and see how you can get your hands on them.

TUNDRA EXPLORATION VEHICLE

SEATS: 2
OBTAIN BY: Purchasing from the Snowy Igloo Shop for 3000 Bucks, or trading

On the 28th of every month, the Snowy Igloo Shop appears near the Playground offering a bunch of frozen goodies. One of those goodies is the Tundra Exploration Vehicle, which makes traversing difficult terrain easy as pie!

DRAGON TRAIN

SEATS: 5
OBTAIN BY: Trading only

The Dragon Train is a long vehicle in the shape of a Chinese dragon, which was released as part of the Lunar New Year event in 2022. It was on sale for 10,500 Bucks at the time, making it the most expensive vehicle in Adopt Me!

YELLOW TAXI CAB

SEATS: 2
OBTAIN BY: Purchasing the Taxi Driver Bundle for R$ 350, or trading

This might seem like an ordinary vehicle, but it's also a route to bundles of Bucks! Other players can request a lift from you when you're driving the Cab, so you can make money as you're exploring!

BUBBLE CAR

SEATS: 4
OBTAIN BY: Purchasing the Ultra Car Pack for R$ 800, or trading

Take a step into the future with the curvy Bubble Car. It can fit four people or pets under its giant domed windows, so everyone gets a great view of the journey.

GYROCOPTER

SEATS: 2
OBTAIN BY: Trading only

Smash together a car and a helicopter and you might end up with something like this Gyrocopter. You can only get your hands on the crazy flying machine by trading now that Rich no longer sells it.

HOVERCRAFT

SEATS: 2
OBTAIN BY: Purchasing for 65 Stars in Star Rewards, or trading

The Hovercraft has a giant inflatable base that lifts it off the ground and a huge fan that propels it around town. You can get it for free once you've collected 65 Stars!

RAINBOW TRAIL MAGIC CARPET

SEATS: 1
OBTAIN BY: Trading only

This Magic Carpet was released as part of the Pride event and was available for only 250 Bucks. It lets you float along at an easy pace, leaving a rainbow trail behind as you go.

IMAGINATION BOX

SEATS: 2
OBTAIN BY: Opening a Gift, or trading

Using your creativity is absolutely free. The Imagination Box will get you around just like any other vehicle, but close your eyes and it can be anything from a speedy racing car to a jumbo jet.

SMART TRADER

Once you've spent a bit of time on Adoption Island, you might find you've got some duplicate pets and items. Instead of letting them go to waste, you can trade with other players to fill the gaps in your collection.

SAFETY FIRST

Before you make your first trade, it would be smart to visit the Safety Hub on the Northmost point of the island, behind Green Groceries. Here you can learn about how to trade safely and take the Trade License Test to prove your skills.

SOMETHING FISHY

Talk to Agent Alex and the test will begin. You'll be shown three trade scenarios, and you have to decide whether they're either a scam or safe, by jumping on the red scam button or the green safe one. Don't worry if you get one wrong—that's how you learn, and you can retake the test.

LICENSED TO TRADE

Once you've answered three questions correctly, you can pick up the Trade License item. This item stays in your backpack and shows off all your recent trades, as well as granting you the ability to trade with and for Ultra-Rare and Legendary items!

TRADING 101

When you're ready to trade, you can approach anyone on the island and select them to bring up the interaction options. If you select Trade, it will bring up the trading window, which looks like this:

CHAT WINDOW
This will let you talk to the other person and discuss the trade before you start loading items into the trade.

OFFERED ITEMS
This side of the trade window shows you what items you've already added to the trade. You can add up to nine items per trade.

RECEIVED ITEMS
The right side of the trade window shows you the items that the other person wants to trade. You'll receive these when both of you accept the trade.

ADD ITEM
This button will bring up your backpack and let you select any of the items that you own to add to the trade.

DECLINE BUTTON
If you think the trade isn't fair, you can cancel the deal by pressing this button.

CONFIRM TRADE

Once you've pressed Accept, it'll bring up an extra confirmation window that asks "Is This Trade Fair?". Take this as a second opportunity to assess the deal before either confirming or declining the trade. If both people accept, then the items are traded and you've got new stuff in your collection!

53

POOL PARTY!

On those hot summer days, there's nothing better than taking a plunge in a cool, refreshing pool. Luckily, Adoption Island has one of the best pools in the universe! Grab your buddies, put on your swimsuit and cannonball in!

MULTI POOL

You can spot the Pool area in the distance by looking out for the giant flamingos, or the huge aquarium wall beside the Pool Shop building. It's made up of lots of interconnected pools, that you can float, swim, or dive in.

PARTY TIME

Your pets love to go for a splash too—even the ones that don't live in the water! Every so often they'll get the Pool Party ailment, which can only be relieved by a nice dip in the water around the Pool Shop. There are dozens of toys, floaties, and water cannons to play with too if you don't want to get soaked straight away!

POOL PETS

That giant aquarium set into the wall might give you a hankering for a fishy friend. Thank goodness then that the Pool Shop has you covered. You can buy yourself a Rare Goldfish pet for 1400 Bucks, or even get a pair of unusual Sand Dollars for R$ 240!

WATER WINGS

💲 50

You can have peace of mind that you're not going to sink while wearing these Water Wings.

FLOATIE RAFT

💲 75

Relax as you laze on the water with the Floatie Raft. How many pets can you fit on before it starts to sink?

PARTY INNERTUBE

💲 150

The perfect equipment for floating along a lazy river. The only struggle you might have is falling through the hole in the middle.

PARTY MERMAID FLOAT

💲 200

If the Party Innertube isn't magical enough for you, this floating fun donut has a flappy blue tail modeled on a mermaid.

PARTY PIZZA FLOAT

💲 300

It's a very dangerous idea to have an inflatable device that looks so tasty. Watch out for hungry pets!

PARTY SURFBOARD

💲 600

The Party Surfboard can be controlled so you can smoothly carve a path around the water.

55

NIGHT IN THE WOODS

There's no better way to enjoy the island than to spend a night under the stars in the wilderness. Head on down to the Campsite with your pets and your pals to enjoy fireside stories, sing-alongs, and delicious camping treats.

PITCH PERFECT

You'll find the Campsite on the edge of Adoption Island by the cliff, close to Green Groceries. You don't even have to pack for this camping trip as you can sleep in one of the tents dotted around the site!

GATHER AROUND

The main area of the site is the campfire, which is where you can toast your marshmallows or chill out on the log benches. It's the perfect place to meet your friends and tell spooky stories, or jam with your favorite musical instruments.

THE GREAT OUTDOORS

Even your pet friends know how exciting a camping trip can be, because every so often they'll be struck with the Camping ailment. The only way to satisfy your pet's craving is to visit the Campsite and spend a night in nature.

LODGERS

You can rent the Camping Lodge for 200 Bucks. It has free marshmallows and a shower that you can use in the morning ... but only if your pet has just got rid of the Camping status.

CAMPING SOUVENIRS

You'll find a Camping Shop a short walk away from the main Campsite, which sells equipment that you can use at the Campsite, or to camp anywhere on Adoption Island!

MARSHMALLOWS
💲 0

No camping trip would be complete without toasting marshmallows on an open fire, and the Camping Shop offers them up for free!

FLASHLIGHT
💲 30

If the woods are getting a bit spooky after you've heard scary stories, then the flashlight will let you check that nothing is lurking in the trees ...

GUITAR
💲 500

With no electricity to power modern gadgets, your entertainment will come from a six-stringed guitar! The shop sells a bongo drum if you prefer percussion!

SLEEPING BAG
💲 1000

You don't have to limit sleeping in the great outdoors to the Campsite. The Camper's Sleeping Bag will let your pet sleep anywhere you place it!

TENT
💲 1200

Get protection from the elements while you're camping away from the site by splashing out on the tent.

CAMPING VAN
💲 3000

If you want to travel to the best camping spot, the Camping Van is the perfect vehicle to get you and your pet pal there.

MAKING FUN

As well as keeping your pet pals well-fed and healthy, you've got to have some fun with them too! If you head down to the Toy Shop, you can get your hands on great items to play with. Let's see what's on offer!

FUN FOR SALE

FLOPPY BUNNY PLUSHIE
$ 60

This cute bunny is available on the cheap and offers the warmest, fuzziest cuddles.

STAR BALLOON
$ 120

Grab hold of this balloon and it'll let you jump much higher than normal.

STANDARD UNICYCLE
$ 120

If you've got incredible balance, the Standard Unicycle will let you get around town quicker.

STANDARD POGO
$ 150

If bouncing around like a kangaroo is more your thing, then pick up the Standard Pogo.

STANDARD ROLLER SKATES
$ 300

The coolest mode of transport in the Toy Shop lets you zip around town on your own personal set of wheels.

SPINNING PROPELLER
$ 1300

Don't let go of the Spinning Propeller because once you use it, you'll keep floating into the air.

STANDARD GRAPPLING HOOK
$ 2000

Launch yourself toward any point you aim at by shooting the Standard Grappling Hook.

TOY TOWN

Of course the Toy Shop is the best place to get your hands on an awesome toy, but it's by no means the ONLY place. In fact, you can find toys all around Adoption Island, as long as you know where—and when—to look.

BABY SHOP

If you're playing as a child, or are taking care of one, then the Baby Shop has a selection of rattles that can keep kids entertained. Most of them are modeled after the pets that you can take care of too!

DESERT SHOP

Once a month, the waters of the river subside near the school and a desert location appears, including the Desert Shop, which has some toys themed around the arid environment.

SNOWY IGLOO SHOP

This icy shop also appears once a month (on the 28th) but freezes over the river by the Playground instead. It offers frosty pets, vehicles, and toys.

FALL SHOP

When the leaves start turning brown on the 20th of each month, visit the Fall Shop. Its stock includes the Finger Piano, as well as some delicious autumnal foods!

RAIN GIFT SHOP

A rainy day makes the Rain Gift Shop appear at the Campsite. It has some watery toys for sale on the 23rd of each month, including the awesome Grapplenana and adorable Pirate Plushie.

SEASONAL EVENTS

Keep your eyes peeled every day of the year, because if there's an event going on, there are always a few new toys on offer. Previous events have given us the Zombie Finger Rattle and the Snowball Launcher.

59

PLAYTIME!

Sadly we're on the final stop of our tour around Adoption Island, but never fear—we've saved the best until last. The Playground is where everybody comes to have fun, play with their pals, and keep boredom at bay!

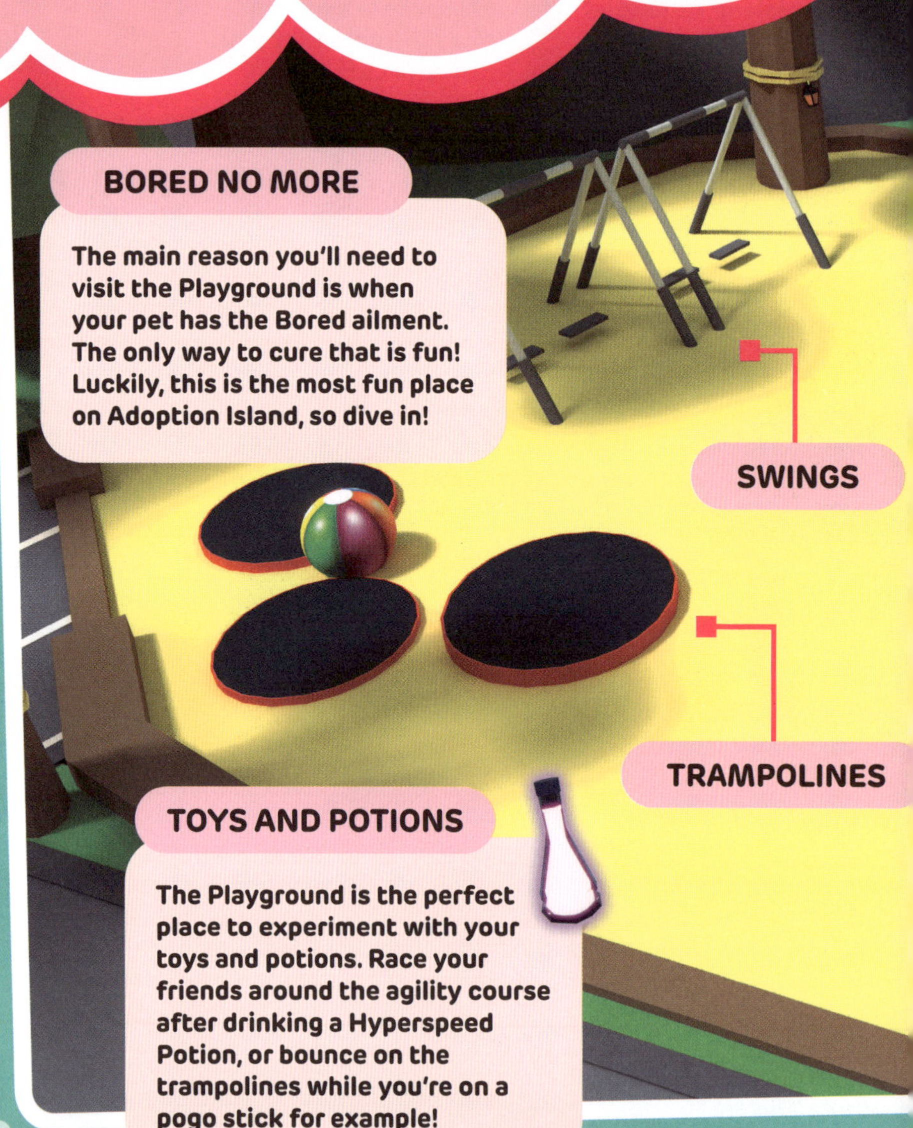

BORED NO MORE

The main reason you'll need to visit the Playground is when your pet has the Bored ailment. The only way to cure that is fun! Luckily, this is the most fun place on Adoption Island, so dive in!

SWINGS

TRAMPOLINES

TOYS AND POTIONS

The Playground is the perfect place to experiment with your toys and potions. Race your friends around the agility course after drinking a Hyperspeed Potion, or bounce on the trampolines while you're on a pogo stick for example!

CHALLENGE ACCEPTED

Look for the door at the back of the Playground beside the slide if you want a real challenge. This door leads you to the Obby Lobby, where you can take on one of five tricky courses. Turn to the next page to get a sneak peek at what you'll be up against.

JUMBO SLIDE

SEE-SAW

AGILITY COURSE

MERRY-GO-ROUND

PUTTING ON A SHOW

There's a giant decked area behind the jumbo slide that's perfect for a performance. Whether you want to host a pet fashion show, or act out a play with your pals, the stage is the ideal place to gather.

OBBY LOBBY

If you decided to go through the door at the back of the Playground, then you'll be faced with a series of portals that transport you to obby courses of increasing difficulty. Do you have what it takes to complete them all?

MINIWORLD

The easiest of the obbies puts you in a giant bedroom—or maybe the portal shrunk you down to miniature size ... Either way, you've got to cross the room, climb onto the bed, and make a leap of faith to reach the finish.

Difficulty: ●○○○○○○○○○

LONELY PEAK

Take a trip above the clouds for the Lonely Peak obby. You'll need to brave a series of sheer cliffs, navigate rope ladders, and climb even higher up the mountain to end the course safely. Just don't look down!

Difficulty: ●●○○○○○○○○

COASTAL CLIMB

Don't be fooled by the pleasant grassy surroundings: the Coastal Climb is a tricky course that will have you bouncing on barrels and climbing crates to reach the finish high upon the forest canopy.

Difficulty: ●●●○○○○○○○

SHIPWRECK BAY

Down by the water, the ruins of a ship signal the start to this tricky obby. If you have your sea legs on and can skillfully navigate the wreckage and cliffside houses, you'll be the pirate king or queen of Shipwreck Bay.

Difficulty: ●●●●○○○○○○

ANCIENT RUINS

This place has seen better days. Suspended above a boiling pit of lava, the Ancient Ruins obby is packed with weird, winding pathways that take you higher and higher until you reach the spiral staircase at the end.

Difficulty: ●●●●●○○○○○

PYRAMID

More lava! But at least the Pyramid obby doesn't also have you battling heights too. This challenging course is more focused on precise leaps between small platforms across the glowing magma.

Difficulty: ●●●●●●○○○○

TINY ISLES

Now if you're looking for a real challenge, Tiny Isles is the place to go. You might not even be able to find the first obstacles, let alone manage to beat them! This map is for pro parkour people only.

Difficulty: ●●●●●●●●●●

63

Hello again, human!

I hope that you've enjoyed your guided tour around the hotspots of Adoption Island. Isn't there just so much to see and do?

By now you'll have met the friendly community, collected a couple of pet pals, made a home away from home in the Neighborhood, and visited all the amazing shops too. I dare say your suitcase will be full to the brim with souvenirs. Mostly, however, I hope you've had a truckload of fun, because that's what this place is all about!

You're always welcome to visit again and I've got a sneaking suspicion you'll be back very soon.

Until then, human, farewell!

Sir Woofington